Revolutionizing Your Approach to Selling

Ways to Leverage Social Media for Sales

Tess Adventures

The Dawn of Social Media Sales

Social media sales are changing the way businesses sell their products and services, offering both challenges and opportunities. With the rise of platforms like Facebook, Instagram, and TikTok, selling isn't just about putting products in front of people anymore. It's about engaging with potential customers where they hang out online, as well as using creative ways to grab their attention. As these platforms evolve, how we use them for sales must change too. In this chapter, we'll dive into how social media has transformed modern selling techniques, highlighting its role in creating new strategies that bridge the gap between sellers and consumers in a more interactive and personal way.

We'll explore the evolution of social media's influence on sales from its early days to its current status as a pivotal tool for marketers. You'll see how businesses have moved from merely having an online presence to fully integrating social media into their sales strategies. The journey incorporates everything from establishing a brand's voice, managing public perception through user feedback, to crafting visually appealing content that stops the scroll. We'll also touch on emerging trends like social commerce and influencer marketing, which have redefined how businesses connect with their audiences. Throughout this chapter, we'll provide insights tailored for small business owners, entrepreneurs, and marketing professionals, focusing on cost-effective strategies to boost engagement and sales. Whether you're a newcomer looking to make your mark or a seasoned professional aiming to keep up with digital trends, this exploration offers practical insights to leverage social media effectively.

Historical Overview of Social Media Marketing

The journey of social media marketing is a fascinating narrative of transformation, beginning with the emergence of early social networking sites such as MySpace and Friendster. In the late 1990s and early 2000s, these platforms revolutionized the way people connect online, setting the foundation for what we see today. MySpace, with its customizable profiles and music playlists, was more than just a hub for personal connections; it became a fertile ground for artists and businesses to tap into new audiences. Friendster, though less commercially successful, hinted at the potential reach and influence of social networks. This period marked the first tentative steps toward leveraging online communities for marketing purposes. As these sites grew in popularity, companies began experimenting with their capabilities, albeit in rudimentary ways. The focus was on gathering followers and friends, laying the groundwork for more sophisticated strategies.

As time progressed, social media's role evolved from being purely personal to an indispensable tool for dynamic business engagement. This transition was fueled by the explosive growth of Facebook around 2004, which introduced features that appealed both to individuals wanting to connect personally and businesses seeking new marketing avenues. Businesses started using Facebook pages to engage directly with users, share content, and build relationships. This change represented a significant shift in how brands interacted with consumers, moving away from traditional broadcast advertising to more interactive, two-way communication. It enabled companies to personalize their interactions and foster communities around their brands, thereby deepening customer relationships. This era also gave rise to targeted advertising, allowing businesses to reach specific demographics more effectively than ever before.

Another crucial development in social media marketing was the rise of user reviews and social feedback, profoundly influencing brand perception. Unlike traditional forms of advertising, where brands had full control over the message, social media shifted some of that power to consumers. Reviews, ratings, and comments became public forums for customers to express their opinions. This transparency brought about 'social proof,' where potential buyers would look to the experiences of others before making a purchase decision. Companies quickly learned the importance of managing their online reputation, responding to reviews, and engaging with customers to maintain a positive image. Social proof became a powerful marketing tactic, offering credibility and authenticity that traditional marketing struggles to match.

In tandem with these changes was the evolution of content strategy on social media. Initially dominated by static, text-based updates, platforms soon recognized the growing appetite for multimedia content. Instagram and Pinterest, launched around 2010, emphasized visual storytelling, using images and videos to captivate audiences. Brands began shifting their content strategies to focus on visually appealing materials, knowing that attention spans were short and visuals could communicate messages quickly and effectively. Multimedia content strategies allowed businesses to showcase products in use, highlight customer testimonials, or provide behind-the-scenes looks at their operations. Such engaging content not only attracted larger audiences but also fostered emotional connections with them. As technology advanced, video content gained prominence, driven by YouTube and later TikTok. These platforms demonstrated the power of video to entertain, educate, and inspire, leading to the creation of tutorials, product demonstrations, and even viral challenges that significantly boosted brand visibility.

The success of social media marketing lies in its ability to adapt to changing consumer preferences and technological advancements. Over time, it has become essential for modern selling techniques, helping businesses reach their target markets more efficiently and cost-effectively. For small business owners and entrepreneurs, especially those with limited budgets, social media offers a valuable platform to establish a brand presence and engage directly with customers. With tools like analytic insights, businesses can tailor their strategies, continuously refining their approaches based on performance metrics.

Yet, amid all this evolution, there remains a constant – the need for authenticity. Users crave genuine interactions and personalized experiences that resonate on a deeper level. Successful social media marketers understand this and strive to create meaningful content that aligns with their audience's values and interests. Whether through compelling storytelling, user-generated content, or real-time engagement, brands must maintain a balance between promotional efforts and authentic connections.

Key Trends Shaping Digital Sales Today

In recent years, social media has revolutionized the way businesses engage in sales, particularly through emerging trends that are reshaping digital commerce. A pivotal trend is the surge in mobile commerce, largely facilitated by social media platforms. With smartphones becoming ubiquitous, consumers increasingly prefer shopping via their mobile devices. This shift necessitates that businesses optimize their sales strategies for mobile interfaces to remain competitive. If your business isn't mobile-friendly, potential sales might be slipping through your fingers.

It's essential to ensure websites and online stores are not just accessible but also visually appealing and easy to navigate on smaller screens. Emphasize features like quick loading times, intuitive designs, and simple checkout processes. Mobile optimization isn't just about technology; it's about understanding consumer behavior and providing a seamless shopping experience that keeps customers coming back.

Influencer marketing is another significant trend that can't be ignored. Influencers have become modern-day brand ambassadors who wield considerable power in increasing brand visibility, especially within niche markets. The allure of influencers lies in their ability to build trust with their followers, making their product recommendations more impactful than traditional advertising methods. Collaborating with influencers allows brands to tap into pre-built networks of engaged audiences. When an influencer shares a positive experience with a product, it can resonate deeply with their followers, driving interest and sales. For small businesses, partnering with micro-influencers—those with smaller, highly engaged audiences—can be both cost-effective and incredibly rewarding.

User-generated content (UGC) is equally transformative, offering brands a way to enhance authenticity while lowering production costs. UGC involves consumers creating content that showcases their experiences with a brand, such as reviews, photos, or videos. What makes UGC special is its genuine nature. It's seen as more trustworthy compared to traditional advertisements since it's created by real customers rather than the brand itself. Encouraging customers to share their experiences not only fosters a sense of community but also builds credibility. Brands can initiate UGC campaigns by inviting customers to post testimonials, unboxing videos, or creative uses of their products. This type of content can bolster brand authenticity, increase engagement, and even sway potential buyers' perceptions positively. Additionally, reposting and engaging with UGC amplifies a brand's reach while nurturing a loyal and involved customer base (Yuen, 2024).

Integrating social commerce with shopping experiences through features like shoppable posts within apps is another key development. Social commerce seamlessly marries social media with e-commerce, allowing consumers to make purchases directly from within a social platform. This approach provides a frictionless shopping experience, which is crucial in today's fast-paced digital world. For small businesses, integrating social commerce offers an opportunity to leverage the built-in user bases of social media platforms without the need for extensive investment in standalone e-commerce infrastructure. Features like Instagram's shoppable posts or Facebook's marketplace mean businesses can turn casual browsing into sales opportunities directly within the app. The implications of this for small businesses are profound. Not only can it significantly widen exposure, but it also simplifies the path to purchase, making it easier for spontaneous buys.

Moreover, social commerce isn't restricted by demographic boundaries. While younger generations led the charge in adopting these shopping habits, older generations are catching up. Studies show that people across all generations are engaging in social commerce, debunking the myth that social media sales are only for a younger audience (<i>What Is Social Commerce? Trends and Statistics to Know</i>, 2016). As platforms refine their e-commerce tools, they provide marketers with more data-driven insights, allowing for personalized marketing strategies that can target specific audience segments effectively.

Summary and Reflections

Reflecting on the journey we've explored in this chapter, it's clear how social media has transformed the way businesses sell today. From the early days of MySpace and Friendster to the dynamic world of Facebook and Instagram, each platform has played a role in shaping marketing strategies. We've seen the shift from basic online communities to vibrant spaces where brands can engage with audiences more personally and authentically. Small business owners can truly benefit from these platforms, as they provide innovative ways to reach potential customers without breaking the bank. By tapping into trends like influencer partnerships and user-generated content, businesses can build trust and expand their reach effectively.

Looking ahead, it's evident that social media is not just a trend but an essential tool for modern selling techniques. As technology continues to advance, so too does the opportunity for businesses to connect with their audience in new, meaningful ways. With mobile commerce becoming ever-important and social commerce integrating shopping directly into social experiences, the path to purchase is smoother than ever. For entrepreneurs and small businesses, keeping abreast of these shifts is critical. By staying informed and adapting strategies to include mobile-friendly designs, engaging content, and authentic interactions, companies can maintain a competitive edge. Social media offers a playground of possibilities; it's up to you to leverage it for growth and success.

Reference List

Boyd, D., & Ellison, N. (2010). *Social Network sites: definition, history, and Scholarship*. IEEE Engineering Management Review.

The. (2024). *The Evolution Of Social Media Marketing - FasterCapital*. FasterCapital. https://fastercapital.com/topics/the-evolution-of-social-media-marketing.html

What is Social Commerce? Trends and Statistics To Know. (2016). Shopify Plus. https://www.shopify.com/enterprise/blog/social-commerce-trends

Yuen, M. (2024, January 17). *Guide to social commerce and the evolving path to purchase*. EMARKETER. https://www.emarketer.com/insights/social-commerce-brand-trends-marketing-strategies/

Choosing the Right Platform

Choosing the Right Platform

Choosing the right platform is key for any small business aiming to master social media. With so many options out there, finding the one that aligns with your needs can feel overwhelming. Each social media channel offers something unique—some are great for visuals, others for real-time communication. But before diving in headfirst, it's crucial to understand where your target audience hangs out and what kind of interaction they're looking for. This isn't just about following trends; it's about strategic thinking that considers both your business goals and your audience's preferences.

In this chapter, we'll explore various factors that influence the selection of a social media platform and how they interact with your broader business strategy. We'll delve into understanding your audience's demographics and behaviors, which can guide you in choosing a platform that'll give you the best chance of connecting with them effectively. These insights will help you create engaging content that not only captures attention but also fosters loyalty. Furthermore, we'll discuss aligning platform choices with specific business objectives, whether it's brand awareness, customer service, or community building. Finally, we'll address the practical considerations like budget management and resource allocation, ensuring you get the most bang for your buck without spreading yourself too thin. By the end of this chapter, you'll have a clearer picture of how to navigate the dynamic digital landscape and make informed decisions that align with your growth goals.

Factors Influencing Platform Selection

Unlocking the potential of social media can be a game-changer for small businesses seeking to boost their online presence and engagement. However, choosing the right platform requires strategic thinking and understanding your business's unique goals and audience characteristics. Let's dive into how you can make informed choices aligned with your strategies and objectives.

When selecting a social media platform, start by examining your target audience's characteristics. It's crucial to understand where your audience spends most of their time online. By identifying these platforms, you can create more engaging content that resonates with them. Conducting audience research is a great first step. You might consider using customer surveys or tools like Google Analytics to gain insights into demographics and user behavior—factors like age, gender, interests, and even geographic location play a big role in determining the best platform for your audience. This targeted approach will help you connect with your audience on a deeper level, fostering increased interaction and loyalty. (Digital Marketing Institute, 2024)

Next, align your choice of platform with your business goals. Each social media platform offers distinct features that can support different objectives, such as brand awareness, lead generation, customer service, or community building. For instance, if your goal is to provide top-notch customer support, platforms like Twitter could be effective due to their real-time interaction capabilities. Alternatively, if you're focusing on expanding brand recognition, Instagram's visual appeal might be your go-to due to its strong engagement rates with lifestyle and product brands. Clearly defining what you want to achieve on social media will guide you in selecting the platform whose features best match these goals. Remember, it's about prioritizing the goals that matter most to your growth and success.

Another important factor is content type suitability. Different platforms cater to different types of content—whether visual, textual, or mixed forms. For example, Instagram and Pinterest are ideal for image-centric content, whereas Facebook provides a balanced space for both text and visuals. Meanwhile, LinkedIn is perfect for B2B engagements and thought leadership through detailed articles and professional updates. If your strategy involves video content, platforms like TikTok and YouTube are unmatched in reach and engagement. Evaluating which form of content aligns with your brand's voice and message helps ensure that your efforts are not only seen but also appreciated by your target audience. This approach enhances your storytelling ability, making your brand more relatable and memorable.

Lastly, consider your resources and budget. Managing social media effectively requires time and financial investment, and smaller businesses often face constraints in these areas. Therefore, it's vital to focus your efforts on platforms that offer the highest return on investment (ROI). Assess the cost of creating content, running ads, and maintaining an active presence on each platform against the potential benefits they offer. Tools like analytics and performance metrics can aid in this evaluation, helping you identify which platforms yield the best results for the least cost. Opting for a few well-managed platforms over spreading yourself too thin across many is usually a wiser strategy. This ensures that your limited resources are used efficiently, maximizing impact without stretching your budget too far.

Pros and Cons of Popular Platforms

Navigating the sea of social media platforms to choose the best fit for your small business can feel like quite the adventure. However, by understanding the unique offerings of each platform, you can make strategic decisions that align with your goals and maximize your marketing efforts.

Let's start with Facebook—a longstanding giant in the social media world. With over 3 billion monthly active users, Facebook's extensive reach is unparalleled (Yaeger, 2020). This makes it an excellent choice for businesses looking to reach a wide and diverse audience. One of the key advantages of Facebook is its advanced targeting options. These allow businesses to hone in on specific demographics, interests, and behaviors, ensuring their content reaches the right eyes. Additionally, Facebook's integration with e-commerce solutions such as Facebook Shops can streamline the purchase process, making it easier for consumers to buy directly from the platform. However, while its massive user base is appealing, it's important to remember that engagement on Facebook can vary widely, so crafting compelling, targeted content is crucial.

Shifting gears, Instagram offers a visually-driven environment that can be particularly beneficial for lifestyle and product-based brands. The platform thrives on high-quality photos and videos, making it ideal for showcasing products through aesthetic visuals and captivating storytelling. Instagram Stories and Reels provide businesses with dynamic ways to engage audiences through interactive and ephemeral content, fostering authentic interactions. Given its popularity among younger demographics—especially those aged 18 to 34—the platform is perfect for brands aiming to connect with younger consumers looking for inspiration or new trends (Sprout Social, 2024).

LinkedIn, on the other hand, is the go-to platform for B2B sales and professional networking. It boasts a user base of over 1 billion members across 200 countries, with the United States leading in user count (Sprout Social, 2024). LinkedIn allows businesses to engage within professional circles, offering opportunities for networking and lead generation that are hard to match elsewhere. Its capacity for supporting long-form content makes it the perfect venue for sharing thought leadership pieces that can establish authority in a field. Companies can disseminate industry insights, case studies, and white papers, making LinkedIn invaluable for building a business's reputation and credibility among peers and potential clients.

Now, let's talk about YouTube—an expansive platform dedicated to video content, which serves as a powerful tool for long-term lead generation. YouTube's reach is vast, allowing businesses to tap into a global audience. It's ideal for businesses that have the resources to produce high-quality video content. Whether it's how-to guides, product demonstrations, or engaging storytelling, video content has the potential to captivate viewers, increase brand visibility, and drive subscriptions to a brand's channel. Though creating professional-grade videos requires investment in terms of time and money, the long shelf-life and shareability of YouTube content can yield significant returns over time.

When considering which platform to incorporate into your strategy, think about where your target audience is most active and what type of content you can consistently create. For instance, if your business revolves around photogenic products and a young audience, Instagram might be your top pick. If you're a service-based company targeting professionals, LinkedIn could offer the greatest potential. For any strategy to be successful, it's vital to allocate your budget wisely. As advertising on these platforms grows more competitive, understanding your metrics and return on investment will help in deciding where to focus your efforts (Sprout Social, 2024).

Final Thoughts

Choosing the right social media platform can seem overwhelming, but it's all about understanding where your audience hangs out and how you want to engage with them. By doing a bit of research into your audience's online habits and matching that with your business goals, you can make smarter choices on which platforms to invest in. Whether it's Facebook's wide reach, Instagram's visual flair, LinkedIn's professional network, or YouTube's video dominance, knowing what each platform offers helps you align your content strategy effectively. Don't forget to consider the kind of content you can consistently create and share, as this will drive your engagement and ultimately help your brand stand out.

In addition, remember to factor in your budget and resources. Small businesses often have limited marketing funds, so focusing your efforts on the platforms that promise the best return for your investment is crucial. It's about being strategic—sometimes fewer, well-managed accounts can have a bigger impact than spreading your resources too thinly across multiple channels. Keep an eye on performance metrics to understand what's working and tweak your strategies as needed. With these tips in mind, you're well on your way to crafting a social media presence that resonates with your audience and supports your business growth.

Reference List

Accion Opportunity Fund. (2023). *Choosing the Right Social Media Platform for Your Business*. Accion Opportunity Fund. https://aofund.org/resource/choosing-right-social-media-platform-your-business/

Digital Marketing Institute. (2024, July 19). *Which Social Media Platforms Should You Use for Your Business? | Online Digital Marketing Courses*. Digitalmarketinginstitute.com. https://digitalmarketinginstitute.com/blog/which-social-media-platforms-should-you-use-for-your-business

Sprout Social. (2024, February 8). *50+ of the Most Important Social Media Marketing Statistics for 2023*. Sprout Social. https://sproutsocial.com/insights/social-media-statistics/

Yaeger, A. (2020, June 12). *Advertising On LinkedIn Vs. Facebook, Instagram, Google, And YouTube*. Llama Lead Gen. https://www.llamaleadgen.com/post/advertising-on-linkedin-vs-facebook-instagram-google-and-youtube

Crafting Engaging Content

Crafting Engaging Content

Crafting engaging content is key to capturing the attention of your audience and making a lasting impression. In today's fast-paced digital world, where social media plays a pivotal role in marketing strategies, it's more important than ever to connect with your followers in meaningful ways. This connection isn't just about making people pause as they scroll through countless posts—it's about creating content that speaks directly to them, resonates with their individual experiences, and motivates them to take action. Whether you're sharing a story or an image, each piece of content is an opportunity to build a relationship with your audience.

In this chapter, we delve into the art of developing memorable content that not only reaches but captivates your target market. We'll explore how storytelling can be a powerful tool for engagement, helping you weave narratives that align with your brand's values while drawing your audience closer. On top of that, you'll discover how visual strategies can enhance your storytelling, using platforms like Instagram and Facebook to their full potential without needing a big budget. From creating relatable characters to incorporating effective call-to-actions, the journey in this chapter will equip you with practical insights and techniques. By the end, you'll be well-prepared to implement these strategies, making your social media presence not just noticeable, but truly impactful.

Techniques for Storytelling via Social Media

Understanding and harnessing the power of storytelling is a crucial asset for any brand looking to engage its audience effectively. Storytelling is not just about weaving an interesting tale; it's about crafting a narrative that aligns with your brand's mission and values, creating a bond with your target audience on a deeper emotional level. This connection can drive engagement, loyalty, and even influence purchasing decisions. Diving into the heart of storytelling begins with knowing your brand's narrative inside out. Imagine your brand story as a journey that echoes your company's objectives and ethical stance, breathing life into ideas that your audience cares about. For instance, many successful brands, like Dove, have built their campaigns around stories that emphasize authentic beauty and self-esteem, which deeply resonate with their consumers. Your brand story should aim to evoke similar emotions, making it memorable and distinct in the crowded marketplace.

Next, let's explore how creating relatable characters or personas can boost engagement. These personas could be fictional, representing the ideal customer, or real-life testimonials from satisfied clients. Consider Airbnb's approach; they often feature stories of hosts and guests, showcasing unique travel experiences. By using such narratives, you build characters that reflect your audience's challenges or aspirations, allowing them to see themselves in the story. This strategy not only humanizes your brand but also fosters a stronger connection with your audience, as they feel recognized and understood.

Moving on, incorporating call-to-actions (CTAs) within your storytelling is pivotal. A well-placed CTA can serve as a gentle nudge, guiding your audience towards a decision. It's essential to integrate these prompts seamlessly into your narrative to maintain the story's flow while directing attention to what action you desire from your audience. For example, a success story of a customer achieving results with your product can end with an invitation to try the product themselves, creating urgency and encouraging a prompt response (<i>How to Leverage Emotional Storytelling for Brand Engagement</i>, 2023).

Exploring various storytelling formats is another aspect to consider. Given the myriad of digital platforms available today, each has its uniqueness and strengths. Videos are especially effective due to their ability to merge audio and visual elements, delivering an immersive experience that engages the senses. Brands like Nike utilize powerful visuals and strong narratives in their commercials, striking a chord with their audience across multiple demographics. But don't limit yourself to videos; written posts, live streams, infographics – each medium can amplify different aspects of your story, catering to varied audience preferences. The key is to tailor your format to match the platform and the message you wish to convey.

Incorporating storytelling into your marketing toolkit requires a thoughtful blend of creativity, authenticity, and strategic thinking. As small business owners or budding entrepreneurs, you might wonder how to achieve all this without a hefty budget. The good news is that storytelling doesn't necessarily demand high expenditure. It relies on the sincerity of your message and the originality of your approach. Free tools and user-friendly apps can help you create compelling content without breaking the bank, whether you're designing simple graphics or editing short video clips.

For those who are relatively new to social media marketing, start by observing how others in your industry tell their stories. Notice the emotions they evoke, the characters they build, and the actions they drive. Once you've gathered insights, begin drafting your narratives, perhaps starting with a personal anecdote or a client success story. Over time, with practice and feedback, you'll refine your storytelling skills, ensuring that your brand not only reaches more people but also leaves a lasting impact.

Visual Content Strategies to Increase Engagement

In the digital age, visual content is king, especially on social media. It captures attention quickly and keeps it. For small businesses and startups eyeing cost-effective marketing strategies, understanding the power of visuals in social media engagement can be a game-changer.

First off, high-quality visuals are crucial. Think of them as the face of your brand. Poorly made images or videos can hurt your business's reputation faster than you can say "unfollow." But when you use sharp, high-resolution visuals, they reflect professionalism and build trust with your audience. Quality content also has a higher chance of being shared, boosting your visibility without any extra cost.

Professionalism isn't just about aesthetics; it's about conveying the right message clearly and effectively. Investing in good equipment or hiring a professional can make all the difference. Plus, clear and detailed visuals can enhance the storytelling aspect of your brand, making your posts not just a scroll-by but a stop-and-stare.

Next up, infographics and data visualization are powerful tools for simplifying complex information. By turning dense stats or concepts into visually appealing graphics, you make the content more digestible and shareable. This approach not only helps establish your authority in the field but also improves engagement metrics. Infographics are like shortcuts to understanding—they provide value at a glance which is perfect for the fast-paced world of social media.

Your infographics should align with current trends and interests of your audience. Sharing statistics that matter to them or finding relatable insights encourages them to engage with and share your content. A well-crafted infographic can become a conversation starter and position your business as a thought leader.

Now, let's talk about experimenting with different formats—this is where things get exciting. Platforms like Instagram and Facebook offer various options beyond static images. Carousel posts allow you to tell a cohesive story across several images or compare product features dynamically. This format engages users longer as they swipe through each image, keeping them invested in your narrative.

Short video clips are another dynamic way to capture attention. With apps like TikTok exploding in popularity, short-form videos have shown to drive impressive engagement. They're perfect for showcasing behind-the-scenes glimpses or quick product demos. Live videos, on the other hand, offer real-time interaction and authenticity, fostering deeper connections. They're your chance to connect directly, answer questions, and build community in an unfiltered environment.

Here's a handy guideline: While experimenting, focus on what captivates and feels authentic to your brand. Experimentation doesn't mean random trials; it involves strategic testing to understand what resonates best with your audience. Use analytics tools to monitor performance and tweak your approach accordingly.

Creating shareable content is the ultimate goal. This involves producing visuals that not only look good but resonate with your audience's values or sense of humor. Integrating branded hashtags can help spread your message further. They're like digital breadcrumbs, leading back to your original post and boosting its reach.

User-generated content (UGC) is another golden nugget. When customers share their experiences with your products, it adds layers of authenticity to your brand. Encouraging UGC by running challenges or featuring customer stories can create a sense of community and trust around your products or services. It's like word-of-mouth advertising on steroids.

Bringing It All Together

Connecting with your audience through storytelling and visual strategies isn't just a trend; it's a powerful approach to drive engagement and sales. This chapter has explored how crafting meaningful brand narratives can help capture the hearts of your customers. By creating relatable characters, weaving in compelling call-to-actions, and choosing the right storytelling formats for different platforms, you can enhance your brand's identity and establish a deeper connection with your audience. It's about being genuine and making your audience feel seen, whether through an inspiring customer story or a captivating video that reflects their dreams and challenges.
We've also delved into the importance of top-notch visuals in grabbing attention and building trust. High-quality images and videos serve as the face of your brand, while infographics simplify complex ideas, making them shareable and engaging. Experimenting with various content formats like carousel posts and short video clips can keep your audience interested and coming back for more. Remember, it's not about having a massive budget but using creativity, authenticity, and a dash of strategy to make your content stand out. By leveraging these storytelling and visual techniques, you're well on your way to connecting meaningfully with your audience and driving them toward action.

Reference List

How to leverage emotional storytelling for brand engagement. (2023, August 7). PlayPlay | Blog. https://playplay.com/blog/emotional-storytelling/

Mawhinney, J. (2019). *45 Visual Content Marketing Statistics You Should Know in 2019.* Hubspot.com. https://blog.hubspot.com/marketing/visual-content-marketing-strategy

Merwin, K. (2024, September 6). *The Impact of Visual Content on Social Media Engagement.* Dragonfly Digital Marketing. https://dragonflydm.com/the-impact-of-visual-content-on-social-media-engagement/

The Role of Storytelling in Marketing: How Stories Evoke Emotion and Drive Engagement. (n.d.). Www.upwardspiralgroup.com. https://www.upwardspiralgroup.com/blog/the-role-of-storytelling-in-marketing-how-stories-evoke-emotion-and-drive-engagement

Decoding Algorithms

Decoding Algorithms

Decoding algorithms is like unlocking the secret door to social media success. These behind-the-scenes tech wonders decide what pops up on your feed, what stays hidden, and why some posts go viral while others barely get a glance. Algorithms are basically the unseen puppeteers in our digital lives, orchestrating how content is displayed based on countless factors. They're constantly evolving, adapting to new trends and user behaviors, making them both fascinating and a bit daunting to anyone trying to crack the code for improved online visibility. Social media isn't just about being present anymore; it's about being seen and engaged with, thanks to these often mysterious algorithms.

In this chapter, we dive into how algorithms rank content and why this matters for businesses keen on boosting their online presence. You'll learn about the metrics that influence how posts are prioritized and why engagement is more critical than ever. We'll explore how interaction history plays a role in what makes it to the top of a feed, along with tips on leveraging these insights to foster stronger brand-audience connections. The discussion also extends into the importance of timing, recency, and relevance as key elements in getting noticed. Furthermore, you'll discover how aligning your content strategy with user preferences can enhance engagement. This journey through the intricacies of algorithmic ranks will equip you with the knowledge to make informed decisions and craft strategies that align with these digital gatekeepers, ultimately enhancing your brand's visibility and interaction online.

Understanding How Algorithms Rank Content

In the digital age, social media algorithms play a critical role in determining which content is seen by whom. For small business owners and entrepreneurs looking to harness social media's power for marketing, understanding these algorithms is essential. Let's dive into how these complex systems function and influence content visibility on various platforms.

First up are engagement metrics, crucial indicators that algorithms use to rank content. Imagine you're scrolling through your favorite social media app; what you see largely depends on how others have interacted with similar posts. Algorithms track likes, shares, comments, and even saves, treating them as votes of confidence. The more engagement a post garners, the higher its chances of being pushed up in visibility, reaching a wider audience. For example, if your Instagram post about a new product receives many likes and comments, the algorithm perceives it as valuable and extends its reach beyond your immediate followers. This is why creating engaging content is pivotal; it's not just about posting but sparking interactions.

Social media algorithms also prioritize content based on personal interaction history. If you're frequently liking or commenting on a friend's content, you'll notice more of their posts appearing in your feed. This pattern underscores the importance of building an active community around your brand. By regularly interacting with your audience, you boost your organic reach. Platforms like Facebook and Instagram excel at recognizing patterns in user behavior, promoting content from those users you engage with most. This means that for businesses, establishing meaningful connections with followers can significantly amplify visibility.

Now, let's talk about recency and relevance—two pillars that impact content ranking. Social media thrives on what's new and timely, rewarding those who keep up. Regularly posting current and relevant content positions you favorably in the eyes of algorithms. Suppose there's a trending topic related to your industry; jumping in with insightful posts can increase your chances of being noticed, as algorithms tend to favor fresh content that engages with ongoing conversations. Regular posting ensures your brand remains visible, keeping you at the forefront of users' feeds and maximizing your exposure.

Another interesting aspect is how algorithms adapt to individual user behaviors. Each user's interaction patterns inform the algorithm, tailoring the content they see to match their preferences. For instance, if someone frequently watches DIY videos, they will likely continue seeing similar content. As a small business owner, this means aligning your content strategy with prevalent user habits and preferences. Understanding what resonates with your audience allows you to create content that naturally fits into their feed, increasing the likelihood of engagement. By analyzing insights and feedback, you can refine your approach to mirror the interests of your target audience better.

These elements underscore the dynamic nature of social media algorithms. They are not static rules but ever-evolving guidelines shaped by technology and user interaction. Staying informed about these shifts is vital for leveraging social media effectively. Engagement remains the cornerstone of success, serving as the fundamental metric algorithms use to elevate content visibility. Meanwhile, maintaining consistent, relevant, and interactive content builds rapport with your audience, ensuring your brand stays prominent amidst the constant flow of digital information.

Strategies to Work With Algorithms for Increased Reach

Navigating the world of social media algorithms can seem daunting, especially for small business owners and entrepreneurs looking to amplify their online presence. However, with a strategic approach to content production, you can align your efforts with algorithm preferences to boost visibility and engagement. Let's dive into some actionable strategies that can help you achieve this.

First, understanding when to post is crucial. Posting at times when your audience is most active can significantly enhance immediate engagement. Social media platforms like Instagram and Facebook have analytical tools that reveal the peak activity periods of your followers. For instance, mid-mornings on weekdays tend to be high-traffic times across various platforms. These insights allow you to time your posts for maximum impact. Keep in mind that while general trends provide a starting point, monitoring your specific audience's behavior through analytics will refine the timing even further. Regularly reviewing these metrics helps you adjust your schedule as needed, maintaining consistency without missing changing patterns of engagement (This Is the Best Time to Post on Instagram (and Other Tips), n.d.).

Engagement-driven content creation can also boost interactions and keep audiences intrigued. Keeping your audience actively involved can take many forms, such as posing questions, running polls, or leveraging storytelling through your posts. This interactive content encourages users to comment, share, and react, which signals algorithms to increase your content's visibility. Consider creating shareable content like infographics or short videos that resonate with your audience's interests. Emphasizing user-generated content can also foster a sense of community around your brand. By highlighting customer testimonials or showcasing how customers use your products, you invite your audience to participate in your story, essentially creating organic ambassadors for your brand.

A deep dive into analytics is invaluable for understanding what works and what doesn't. Platforms like Instagram Insights and third-party tools such as Brandwatch offer robust data sets that enable you to track performance metrics over time. This data provides clarity on which types of content receive the most engagement and when shifts occur. Armed with this information, you can make informed decisions to refine and evolve your strategy continuously. For example, if you notice that video content consistently outperforms static images, an adjustment toward more dynamic visual content could yield better results. This kind of agility ensures that you remain attuned to the constantly evolving nature of audience preferences and platform algorithms (Sprout Social, 2024).

Hashtags are another powerful tool in extending reach and attracting targeted audiences. An effective hashtag strategy involves striking a balance between popular and niche hashtags. While widely used hashtags can increase the chances of your content being seen by a larger audience, they also come with more competition. Conversely, niche hashtags may connect you with a more specific and engaged audience, albeit smaller in number. Experimenting with a mix of both allows you to gauge their effectiveness and adjust accordingly. Also, researching trending hashtags related to your industry can provide opportunities to join wider conversations and increase your posts' discoverability.

Incorporating these strategies requires ongoing attention and adaptation. As you build your social media presence, it's important to remember that the key to thriving is not just about playing the algorithm game but about authenticity and providing value to your audience. The more genuine and relatable your content feels, the more likely it is to engage people naturally. Adjustments in your strategy should always circle back to what resonates most effectively with your audience.

Bringing It All Together

In this chapter, we've explored how social media algorithms impact the visibility of business content online. By understanding key elements like engagement metrics and personal history, you can effectively navigate these systems to maximize your reach. Remember, it's about more than just posting; it's about creating engaging, relevant content that sparks interaction. Staying updated on algorithm changes and adapting your strategy is crucial for standing out in the crowded digital space.
We've also discussed practical strategies to work alongside these algorithms. Timing your posts for peak activity and crafting content that invites interaction can significantly boost visibility. Don't forget the power of analytics in refining your approach—insights are your best friend here! Alongside this, leveraging both popular and niche hashtags can help increase discoverability without getting lost in the noise. As you continue building your social media presence, keep focusing on authenticity and delivering value to your audience.

Reference List

Adisa, D. (2023, October 30). *Everything you need to know about social media algorithms*. Sprout Social. https://sproutsocial.com/insights/social-media-algorithms/

Iqbal, S. (2024, May 28). *How Social Media Algorithms Affect Content Visibility*. Content Whale. https://content-whale.com/blog/impact-of-social-media-algorithms-on-content-visibility/

Sprout Social. (2024, April 10). *The best times to post on social media in 2024*. Sprout Social. https://sproutsocial.com/insights/best-times-to-post-on-social-media/

This is the Best Time to Post on Instagram (and Other Tips). (n.d.). Brandwatch. https://www.brandwatch.com/blog/best-time-to-post-on-instagram/

Building a Community Online

Building a Community Online

Building a community online goes beyond just gathering followers; it's about creating a space where engagement, loyalty, and creativity thrive. When small business owners and startups start investing in their online communities, they lay the foundation for not just a customer base but a supportive network that can drive organic growth. This chapter navigates how fostering a vibrant community online can make a significant difference in your brand's success. It's not about the size of the community but the quality of interaction and the genuine relationships formed. Here, we'll delve into the strategies that can transform your social media presence from just another feed into a bustling hub of activity where people feel valued and heard.

You'll discover how engaging with your audience is like having an ongoing conversation that deepens emotional ties, boosting customer loyalty. We'll explore why communication shouldn't be one-sided, highlighting the power of regular interactions like personalized messages and thoughtful responses to comments. The focus will then shift to how organizing virtual events can offer unique experiences that bond community members more closely to your brand. There's a section on creating interactive content, such as polls or quizzes, which not only increases participation but also broadens your reach as participants share within their networks. Finally, we'll discuss how consistent communication through different channels keeps your community updated and invested in your story. Whether you're a small business with a tight budget or a startup trying to break through the noise, this practical guide will equip you with insights to harness the potential of your online community effectively.

Engagement and Loyalty through Community Interactions

Engaging with your audience is a vital strategy for building emotional connections, which in turn enhances customer loyalty and increases repeat sales. When customers feel emotionally connected to a brand, they are more likely to return for future purchases. Think of engagement as having an ongoing conversation with your customers, one that makes them feel valued and understood. This can be achieved through personalized emails, interactive social media content, or even simple things like responding thoughtfully to comments. These interactions show that you care about their opinions and needs, creating a strong emotional bond that encourages customers to stick around.

Another critical aspect of maintaining customer loyalty and driving sales is establishing regular communication with your community. Keeping your audience informed and involved ensures that your brand remains at the forefront of their minds. Regular updates—whether through newsletters, blog posts, or social media—help keep your community engaged, making them more likely to choose your products over competitors. Consistent interaction fosters familiarity, which naturally breeds trust. This strategy not only reinforces your brand's presence but also nurtures a reliable customer base that contributes to organic growth.

Encouraging feedback from your community plays a pivotal role in showing customers that their opinions matter. When people see that their input has a real impact—be it in product development or service improvements—they tend to develop a deeper sense of loyalty towards the brand. Soliciting feedback can be done through surveys, reviews, or direct messages. By actively seeking and implementing customer suggestions, businesses can tailor their offerings more closely to what customers want. This process not only refines products but also strengthens the trust between a brand and its community, fostering an environment where customers feel heard and appreciated.

Organizing online events is another effective way to foster a sense of belonging among your community members. Virtual meetups, live streams, or webinars can create memorable experiences that connect individuals with your brand on a deeper level. Such events offer opportunities for customers to interact with each other and the business, enhancing their overall experience. By hosting these online gatherings, businesses can strengthen their community bonds and offer unique value beyond just their products. This sense of belonging often translates into increased sales, as customers who feel valued and part of a community are more likely to support the brand repeatedly.

Interactive posts, like polls or quizzes, encourage participation and increase visibility. Sharing these types of content invites your community to engage, providing a platform for them to express their thoughts and preferences. This approach not only boosts engagement but also extends your reach as participants share these interactions within their networks. A practical way to execute this is by asking straightforward questions that invite easy responses. For example, a clothing retailer might post a poll asking which style customers prefer for an upcoming collection, thereby directly involving their audience in the decision-making process.

Creating consistent touchpoints through various channels is essential for keeping your community updated. It's not just about communicating frequently, but doing so meaningfully. For instance, social media platforms offer quick, informal ways to connect, whereas email newsletters can provide more detailed insights into new arrivals or company news. Each platform offers different opportunities to tailor messages according to the medium, enabling you to maintain a dynamic and engaging relationship with your community.

Regular updates ensure your audience feels looped into your brand's story. This doesn't mean bombarding them with information but rather sharing well-timed and relevant content. Whether it's a sneak peek of a new product, behind-the-scenes glimpses of how your team works, or exclusive offers for upcoming launches, these updates keep your audience excited and eager to engage. The secret here lies in balancing frequency with relevance, ensuring every piece of content adds value to your community.

Creating User-Generated Content Opportunities

User-generated content (UGC) plays a crucial role in boosting brand visibility and authenticity. By encouraging customers to share their experiences, brands can create a wealth of content that resonates with potential buyers on a personal level. To make the most out of UGC, businesses can implement several strategies that not only motivate customers to participate but also enhance the brand's image.
One effective approach is offering incentives like contests or giveaways. These serve as powerful motivators for customers to engage with your brand by creating content featuring your products. When individuals enter a contest or receive a giveaway, they often share their experiences with others, effectively becoming authentic testimonials for your brand. For example, a small business might run a photo contest where participants submit images of themselves using its product. Not only does this generate excitement around the brand, but it also provides genuine user stories that can be shared across social media channels, thus reaching a broader audience.

Another key strategy is sharing customer-generated stories and experiences. By spotlighting these narratives, a brand builds a relatable and engaging storyline that potential customers can connect with. People are more likely to trust recommendations from real users rather than direct advertising from the company itself. This personal connection can significantly influence purchasing decisions and strengthen customer loyalty. For instance, featuring a customer's journey or how a product solved a problem for them makes the brand's story more compelling and trustworthy.

Encouraging the use of branded hashtags is another tactic that helps track and amplify UGC. Hashtags enable brands to easily gather and showcase content, while also fostering a sense of community among users. By creating a unique branded hashtag, a business invites users to join a larger conversation, making them feel part of something bigger. This sense of belonging promotes continued participation, as customers enjoy seeing their contributions highlighted and engaging with others who share similar interests.

Leveraging various social media platforms for cross-platform promotion of UGC is also essential. Each platform offers unique ways to showcase user content, helping to broaden the brand's reach. For instance, a business might feature user photos on Instagram, tweet success stories on Twitter, and share video testimonials on Facebook. This cross-promotion not only reinforces the brand's collaborative image but also ensures that diverse audiences are reached, thus expanding the brand's visibility beyond its immediate followers.

It's important to consider that all these efforts contribute to building an authentic brand narrative. Consumers today crave transparency and genuine interactions with brands. UGC provides an opportunity to meet this demand by showcasing real experiences from actual customers. It breaks down barriers between brands and consumers, creating a dialogue that feels natural and unforced.

Small businesses, especially those with limited marketing budgets, can greatly benefit from focusing on UGC. It offers a cost-effective way to market products and build a loyal customer base without the need for expensive advertising campaigns. Instead, happy customers become advocates, spreading positive word-of-mouth about the brand.

Furthermore, UGC not only enhances engagement but also builds trust and credibility. When people see others endorsing a brand based on their experiences, it adds authenticity that traditional advertisements can't provide. In today's crowded marketplace, where consumers have endless choices, establishing trust is pivotal. Brands that effectively harness UGC often find not just increased sales but a community of loyal customers who are eager to contribute.

Summary and Reflections

Alright, so let's sum up this chapter! Building an online community isn't just about creating a space for your audience to hang out; it's about driving organic sales growth by boosting engagement and loyalty. By keeping the lines of communication open through regular updates and interactions, you create emotional connections with your customers. This makes them more likely to stick around and choose your products over others. Whether through social media feedback or interactive content, these touchpoints ensure your brand stays relevant and trusted, encouraging repeat purchases.

On top of that, user-generated content is like striking gold in the digital world. When customers share their positive experiences with your brand, it adds an authentic layer to your marketing efforts. This kind of content resonates well because it comes from real people, making it easier for potential buyers to connect with. From branded hashtags to customer stories, these strategies not only broaden your reach but also solidify your brand's image as genuine and trustworthy. For small businesses, leveraging these elements can offer a cost-effective boost, turning happy customers into ardent brand advocates.

Reference List

Chatfield, E. (2023, October 18). *Customer vs. community engagement: Know the difference*. Customer Marketing Alliance. https://www.customermarketingalliance.com/customer-vs-community-engagement-know-the-difference/

Fadeaway Marketing. (2024, June 26). *The Importance of Community Engagement in Marketing*. Fadeawaymarketing.com; Fadeaway Marketing. https://www.fadeawaymarketing.com/blogs/whats-new/1274330-the-importance-of-community-engagement-in-marketing

Piga, A. (2024, August 12). *Council Post: The Rise Of User-Generated Content And Its Impact On Brand Loyalty And Affinity*. Forbes. https://www.forbes.com/councils/forbesagencycouncil/2022/09/12/the-rise-of-user-generated-content-and-its-impact-on-brand-loyalty-and-affinity/

Sebastian, R. (2023, September 27). *How User-Generated Content Can Boost Your Brand Authenticity*. Three Girls Media. https://www.threegirlsmedia.com/2023/09/27/how-user-generated-content-can-boost-your-brand-authenticity/

Leverage Analytics for Better Insights

Using analytics to get better insights into your business is a game-changer for small business owners and entrepreneurs. By harnessing the power of data, you can refine your social media strategies and make informed decisions that elevate your brand. As you explore the chapter's insights, imagine gaining a clearer understanding of how each post performs and being able to tweak your tactics in real-time. This approach transforms raw data into valuable guidance without getting bogged down by complexity or jargon. Whether you're just starting out or looking to revamp your strategy, embracing analytics can lead to smarter moves and ultimately higher engagement with your audience.

In this chapter, you'll dive into some key metrics that play crucial roles in evaluating success on social media. Discover why engagement rates, conversion rates, reach versus impressions, and click-through rates are not just numbers but vital indicators of your online performance. Learn how to assess these metrics to gauge what's working and where adjustments might be needed. You'll also explore practical methods like A/B testing to hone your content and strategies further. The chapter discusses how feedback loops can help continuously improve your approach by aligning it with real-time customer preferences and expectations. It's all about using analytics to sharpen your marketing efforts, making them cost-effective while maximizing their impact. So, get ready to unlock the potential of data-driven decisions and see how they can significantly boost your social media presence and sales efforts.

Key Metrics for Evaluating Success

Understanding the right social media metrics can significantly enhance your ability to make informed decisions and boost your business's success. It's crucial to know which metrics matter most for small business owners, entrepreneurs, and marketing professionals as they target engagement, conversions, and reach in their social media strategies.

Starting with engagement rate, this metric is a powerful indicator of how your audience interacts with your content. Engagement includes likes, comments, shares, and mentions—any action that shows your audience is not just seeing your content but actively participating with it. A high engagement rate suggests that people find your content appealing, which could lead to increased brand loyalty. This is essential for building a community around your brand since engaged audiences are more likely to share your content and advocate for your brand. For example, if a business notices that posts featuring customer stories receive higher likes and shares than promotional posts, this insight can shape future content strategies to include more user-generated content. Moreover, comparing your engagement rates with industry averages can offer valuable benchmarks to ensure you're on track with your competitors (Hill, 2024).

Next, let's focus on conversion rate, which holds importance in driving sales. Conversion rate measures how often your social media interactions translate into meaningful actions like sales, sign-ups, or downloads. Tracking this metric helps you identify which campaigns and channels are most effective in converting audience interest into tangible outcomes. For instance, if you notice that Instagram stories lead to more website visits and purchases compared to Facebook ads, you know where to allocate more resources. By understanding the conversion potential of different platforms and types of content, you can tailor your marketing efforts to maximize ROI (West, 2023).

In addition to engagement and conversion rates, understanding reach versus impressions is key. Reach represents the number of unique users who see your content, while impressions indicate the total number of times your content is displayed, regardless of whether it's clicked. Differentiating between these two metrics is crucial for evaluating brand visibility over time. Imagine you post an inspirational quote that gains 100,000 impressions but only reaches 50,000 unique users. This data tells you that some users viewed the post multiple times, suggesting it resonated deeply. Tracking both reach and impressions helps identify content that gains traction and maintains visibility, which is particularly useful for spotting trends and understanding audience behavior.

Finally, we have Click-Through Rate (CTR), an important metric for calls-to-action (CTAs). CTR measures how often people click on links within your posts to access additional information, such as a product page or blog post. A strong CTR indicates that your content is compelling enough to drive further interaction and interest. Suppose you've created a promotional post about a new product launch, and the CTR is higher for posts featuring vivid images compared to text-only updates. This insight reveals the power of visuals in engaging your audience and encourages reevaluation of your messaging strategies. By analyzing CTR, businesses can refine their CTAs and optimize overall content effectiveness to align with audience expectations and preferences.

Integrating these essential metrics into your social media strategy provides actionable insights that aid in refining and optimizing your approach. By focusing on engagement rate, conversion rate, reach versus impressions, and CTR, small business owners and entrepreneurs can better understand their audience and improve their marketing effectiveness. Social media is not just about posting content; it's about creating a dialogue, identifying what works, and adapting based on data-driven insights.

Adjusting Tactics Based on Data Insights

In the ever-evolving world of social media marketing, flexibility and adaptability become crucial for small business owners aiming to leverage data insights effectively. Using analytics, you can derive valuable information allowing your business strategy to remain dynamic, relevant, and audience-focused.

First, identifying trends through data patterns is essential in staying ahead. By recognizing what resonates most with audiences and using historical data, small businesses can forecast future behaviors and preferences, leading to more proactive strategies. For instance, if a particular post style has consistently high engagement, replicating its elements across future campaigns may be beneficial. Such analysis reveals seasonal fluctuations or shifts in audience behavior, making it easier to adjust content and maximize impact. Monitoring these trends allows you to adapt swiftly, capitalize on successful tactics, and address any ineffective ones promptly. Analyzing trends over time offers a macro view of your campaigns' trajectory, akin to assembling a puzzle where each data point fits into the broader picture. Identifying consistent growth in engagement rates might indicate that your content reform efforts align well with audience interests. Conversely, a sharp decline could highlight potential algorithm changes or emerging blind spots in your content that need addressing.

One practical approach to implementing these insights is A/B testing or split testing. This powerful technique enables marketers to compare different versions of a campaign element—such as headlines, images, or calls-to-action—and understand which performs better. For example, if you run an online pet store, you might test two subject lines: "Exclusive Deals Inside!" versus "Limited Offer: Pet Supplies Sale Now!" Splitting your audience and deploying each version helps determine which message entices more clicks. The outcome provides concrete data-backed insights into what drives engagement, allowing you to refine your approach further. This iterative process not only enhances campaign effectiveness but also deepens understanding of audience preferences.

Feedback loops play another vital role by facilitating ongoing communication between businesses and their customers. Implementing regular feedback systems, like surveys or social media polls, enables businesses to align more closely with customer expectations and evolving desires. Feedback loops help refine products and services based on real-time inputs, ensuring offerings stay relevant and competitive. For example, after launching a new product line, soliciting customer opinions about features or pricing can inform necessary adjustments, thus enhancing customer satisfaction and loyalty. By continuously engaging with audiences through feedback mechanisms, you can keep track of changes in consumer preferences and adapt strategies accordingly.

Setting KPI goals informed by past data is crucial to strategic planning and accountability. Clear KPIs guide efforts by providing measurable benchmarks toward achieving marketing objectives. These indicators should align with overarching business goals like building brand awareness, driving engagement, or boosting sales. For instance, if expanding your reach is a priority, setting a specific target for unique monthly visitors would be appropriate. By regularly evaluating performance against these metrics, you can ascertain whether current strategies effectively contribute to desired outcomes. Moreover, past data offers context for establishing realistic yet challenging KPIs in your campaigns, helping refine plans based on successes and areas needing improvement. Constantly reviewing and adjusting KPI benchmarks ensures ongoing alignment with business priorities while fostering transparency and responsibility within the organization.

Strategies for Enhanced User Experience

In the evolving landscape of social media, small business owners and entrepreneurs must focus on using analytics to craft compelling user experiences. This approach ensures that every interaction with potential customers is meaningful and effective.

To start, enhancing user engagement through analytics is crucial. Engagement metrics, like likes, comments, shares, and time spent on content, offer valuable insights into user behavior and preferences. By carefully monitoring these metrics, businesses can determine what resonates most with their audience. This information allows for the tailored adjustment of content strategies, making them more relevant and appealing. For instance, if a spike in interactions is noticed when a business posts behind-the-scenes content, it indicates a preference that can be leveraged to maintain high engagement levels.

Personalization plays an integral role in creating these customized experiences. By leveraging data, businesses can make each user feel valued by offering personalized recommendations, targeted promotions, and curated content that aligns with their interests. When users encounter content that speaks directly to their needs and desires, satisfaction skyrockets, leading to higher retention rates. A study by Epsilon found that 80% of consumers are likelier to engage with brands that provide personalized experiences. Personalization also fosters stronger emotional connections, ultimately building brand loyalty over time.

Predictive analytics takes personalization a step further by anticipating future user behavior. By analyzing historical data and trends, businesses can forecast future customer actions and tailor campaigns accordingly. This foresight enables them to craft targeted marketing strategies that not only align with current user expectations but also anticipate desires they may not yet consciously realize. Brands employ predictive modeling to understand when customers are likely to purchase again, allowing timely promotions that boost conversion rates. This proactive approach is akin to reading the minds of customers, ensuring that the right message reaches them precisely when they're ready to engage.

Nevertheless, while pursuing personalization, it's essential to balance data privacy responsibly. Collecting and utilizing customer data comes with significant ethical considerations. Transparency about how data is collected and used is critical in maintaining trust. Businesses should obtain explicit consent from users before collecting personal information and offer clear explanations regarding how it will enhance their experience. Moreover, individuals should always have the option to modify or withdraw their consent. Ethical use of data not only builds credibility and trust but also prevents potential legal issues arising from non-compliance with regulations like GDPR or CCPA.

To ensure consistent improvement in user experiences, setting up feedback loops is invaluable. Feedback loops serve as real-time systems for capturing customer responses and preferences. They enable businesses to make informed adjustments based on direct user input, aligning offerings with evolving customer needs effectively. An example is implementing a suggestion box feature where users can freely voice their ideas and preferences. The continuous flow of feedback nurtures a culture of responsiveness, keeping brands agile and adaptable to ever-changing market dynamics.

Establishing clear Key Performance Indicator (KPI) goals is vital for measuring success in this analytical endeavor. Setting KPIs related to customer satisfaction, retention rates, or increased engagement provides tangible targets that guide strategic planning. These measurable goals act as benchmarks for evaluating progress and making necessary adjustments. For instance, progress might be gauged through tracking improvements in metrics like click-through rates or average session duration on platforms. Achieving KPI goals signifies alignment between customer expectations and brand delivery, reinforcing strategic effectiveness.

Bringing It All Together

Wrapping up this chapter, it's clear that using analytics tools is a game-changer for anyone looking to boost their social media game. We've talked about key metrics like engagement rates, conversion rates, reach versus impressions, and click-through rates, all vital in figuring out what makes your audience tick. By digging into these numbers, you can tweak your strategies to fit what works best for you and your followers. It's not just about posting; it's about having a real conversation with your audience and letting the data guide you to make smart decisions.

Moving forward, remember that being flexible and responsive to the data at hand is crucial. Whether you're an entrepreneur trying to make a splash or a small business owner wanting to get more bang for your buck, tailoring your approach based on solid data insights can really help you stand out. Don't forget to test different tactics and seek feedback from your audience to keep things fresh and effective. At the end of the day, it's about building strong relationships and adapting continuously to make sure your social media marketing efforts really count.

Reference List

Analyzing Social Media Metrics for Campaign Improvement. (n.d.). Https://Www.theadfirm.net/. https://www.theadfirm.net/analyzing-social-media-metrics-for-campaign-improvement/

Deep Sync. (2024, January 10). *4 Data-Driven Marketing Strategies for Small Businesses - Deep Sync*. Deep Sync. https://deepsync.com/small-business-data-driven-marketing/

Hill, C. (2024, April 11). *The Most Important Social Media Metrics to Track*. Sprout Social. https://sproutsocial.com/insights/social-media-metrics/

LatentView, T. (2023, August 17). *Leveraging Data Science and Analytics for Social Media*. LatentView Analytics. https://www.latentview.com/blog/leveraging-data-science-and-analytics-for-social-media/

West, C. (2023). *19 Social Media Metrics That Really Matter—And How to Track Them*. Hootsuite Social Media Management. https://blog.hootsuite.com/social-media-metrics/

White, D. (2024, October 30). *TechFunnel*. Techfunnel.
https://www.techfunnel.com/martech/predictive-analytics-personalized-customer-journeys/

Influencer Partnerships

Influencer Partnerships

Building partnerships with influencers is like finding the right dance partner—when you match your moves perfectly, it can create a dazzling performance that captivates the audience. It's not just about grabbing any hand that reaches out but choosing someone whose style and rhythm align with your brand's beat. In today's digital age, influencers hold significant power, capable of extending your business's reach to new audiences who are already engaged and interested in similar themes. This partnership isn't just about leveraging popularity; it's about crafting authentic relationships that amplify your message while resonating deeply with potential customers. Think of influencer collaborations as a strategic expansion of your marketing family, bringing in voices that echo your values and engage with your audience on a personal level. By aligning yourself with the right people, you're not only enhancing your visibility but also fostering trust and credibility within your target market.

In this chapter, we'll dive into the "how" of influencer partnerships—starting from identifying those perfect matches who share your brand's ethos to establishing robust connections with them. You'll learn methods to pinpoint influencers who vibe with your brand culture and discover how to assess whether their audience aligns with who you're trying to reach. From there, the chapter will guide you through evaluating critical engagement metrics beyond just follower counts, providing insights into the true influence and interaction levels. As we progress, you'll uncover tools and platforms designed to streamline your search and outreach efforts, ensuring efficiency and effectiveness. We'll explore ways to tailor messages that resonate with influencers' unique styles, paving the way for meaningful and lasting collaborations. Additionally, you'll gain insights into nurturing these relationships over time, allowing creativity and genuine representation to take center stage. By the end of this journey, you'll have all the practical insights and strategies needed to form impactful influencer partnerships that drive growth for your business without draining your resources.

Finding and Connecting with the Right Influencers

When it comes to expanding your business's reach in today's digital world, creating strategic partnerships with the right influencers can make a significant difference. But how exactly do you find those ideal influencers? Identifying and building strong relationships with them is crucial for ensuring that your brand resonates with your target audience—an essential step in successful influencer partnerships.

Firstly, it's important to focus on identifying your ideal influencer. This is someone whose characteristics align closely with your brand values and audience needs. To do this, start by analyzing what your brand stands for. Are you eco-friendly, innovative, or focused on quality craftsmanship? Whichever it may be, your influencer should mirror these attributes. Consider the type of messages they already promote and whether they match your brand's ethos. For example, if you're a company selling sustainable fashion products, an influencer who frequently shares content about eco-friendly living would be a natural fit.

A guideline here would be to create a checklist of values and characteristics that are non-negotiable for your brand's identity. Review potential influencers against this checklist to ensure alignment before moving forward. This will help maintain authenticity and consistency across all marketing efforts.

Next, understanding niche alignment between your business offerings and the influencer's content is key. The idea is to ensure that their existing content aligns well with what your brand offers. This not only optimizes partnership effectiveness but also ensures that the influencer can naturally and genuinely integrate your product into their narrative. For instance, if you run a tech startup that's developed a cutting-edge productivity app, partnering with a tech-review influencer who frequently discusses productivity hacks and new gadgets might be highly beneficial. Their audience is likely interested in similar innovations and would be more receptive to learning about your app.

Moving on to assessing influencer audience demographics, it's vital to confirm that they cater to your intended market. Simply put, the influencer's followers should match your target demographic profiles. If you're targeting young professionals, ensure the influencer isn't reaching predominantly retirees. You can typically access demographic data through social media analytics tools provided by various platforms. Another option is to engage directly with the influencer or their agency to request insights into their follower base, which often includes information like age range, location, interests, and more.

To help guide this process, develop a profile of your ideal customer that includes details such as gender, age range, location, income level, interests, and online behavior. Compare this profile with the influencer's audience demographics to gauge compatibility. It's like matchmaking for businesses – both sides must click for the relationship to flourish.

Evaluating engagement metrics is another critical step in predicting the potential success of your collaboration. Metrics such as likes, comments, shared posts, and even mentions can provide insight into how actively engaged an influencer's audience is. Follower count alone doesn't guarantee impact. Instead, focus on how their audience interacts with their content. A smaller following with high engagement is often more valuable than millions of passive viewers. Users who actively comment and share content are likely to act on recommendations from influencers they trust.

An effective way to calculate an influencer's engagement rate involves dividing the number of relevant comments and shares by their total number of followers. This calculation gives a better sense of their influence potency. High engagement rates typically indicate a loyal and interactive community, one that's likely to respond positively to your brand's message.

Utilizing Influencer Platforms and Outreach

Connecting with influencers effectively can significantly expand a business's reach, making influencer partnerships a game-changer for small enterprises, startups, and marketing professionals. Whether you're aiming to enhance brand awareness, boost sales, or build customer relationships, understanding the nuances of influencer engagement is vital. Here's how you can harness platforms and craft messages to foster meaningful connections with influencers.

Utilizing Influencer Platforms

The digital age offers plenty of tools that simplify the process of finding and collaborating with influencers. Influencer marketing platforms are crucial in streamlining your search, offering access to verified profiles tailored to your niche. Platforms like AspireIQ, Traackr, and GRIN allow users to sort by category, audience reach, engagement rates, and more, ensuring you find an influencer who aligns perfectly with your target market.

These tools save hours of manual searching and reduce the risk of partnering with individuals who may not truly represent your brand vision. With a few clicks, these platforms reveal top influencers' stats, previous collaborations, and even preferred communication methods. This transparency ensures that you are reaching out to the right people efficiently and effectively.

Moreover, leveraging platform features enhances outreach efforts dramatically. Many offer integrated messaging tools, allowing brands to pitch collaboration ideas seamlessly within the platform interface. Some even provide templates, helping those new to influencer marketing to formulate their initial pitches without starting from scratch.

Crafting Compelling Outreach Messages

After identifying potential partners, the next step involves crafting messages that resonate. The key is clarity and brevity. Influencers receive countless messages daily; hence, standing out is pivotal. Start by outlining mutual benefits—what value can both parties gain from the collaboration? For example, if you're a skincare startup, express how an influencer's followers will benefit from genuine reviews of your product, enhancing their beauty routines.

Highlight any unique selling points of your business and how these align with the influencer's content. Doing so immediately establishes a connection, demonstrating how much you've thought about a mutually beneficial relationship rather than sending a generic pitch. Personalization goes beyond just mentioning the influencer's name; it involves showcasing that you've taken time to research their style, previous campaigns, and audience preferences.

Tailoring Messages to Reflect Influencer Style

Tailoring your message requires understanding the influencer's communication style and previous work. It shows genuine interest and enhances the probability of getting a positive response. Look at past campaigns the influencer has been involved in and draw parallels to your own brand. If they've worked with eco-friendly companies before, emphasize your commitment to sustainability.

For instance, suppose you're approaching a fashion influencer known for promoting ethically made clothing. In that case, highlight your brand's ethical manufacturing processes or how your products complement their lifestyle choices. Refer to specific posts or campaigns the influencer has managed successfully, and explain why your product would be a perfect fit for their profile.

Remember, building rapport is as important as the initial outreach. Show appreciation for their work, engage with their content, and maintain consistent communication. These actions demonstrate a willingness to build long-term relationships rather than one-off transactions.

Building Relationships Over Time

Establishing trust and authenticity takes time and dedication. Engaging with influencers is not only about immediate results but also about fostering sustainable partnerships. Regularly interact with their social media content, acknowledging their contribution to your brand's mission. Authentic compliments about the influencer's work help solidify these connections, showing respect and admiration beyond business interests.

Additionally, providing influencers with creative freedom in their strategy allows them to represent your brand authentically. Give them the flexibility to share your product in ways they think will resonate best with their audience. This approach often yields organic and genuine promotions, as influencers know what works best for their followers.

Monitoring and Adjusting Strategies Based on Impact

In today's digital landscape, influencer partnerships can be a game-changer for small businesses and entrepreneurs looking to expand their reach. However, the key to maximizing these partnerships lies in assessing their impact and continually enhancing strategies based on performance data. Let's dive into how you can achieve this effectively.

First, it's essential to measure engagement metrics to gauge the success of your influencer collaborations. Metrics such as likes, shares, comments, and saves serve as indicators of how well your audience is interacting with the content produced by influencers. These metrics help you understand not just how many people are seeing your content, but how they are engaging with it. For instance, a high number of 'saves' might suggest that your content is seen as valuable or inspirational to your audience. By routinely analyzing these engagement figures, you can assess if your campaigns are hitting the mark or need tweaking.

Next up is gathering customer feedback, which offers direct insight into shifts in brand perception following an influencer campaign. You can employ surveys to collect structured feedback regarding opinions and experiences with your brand. Additionally, social media sentiment analysis tools can track what consumers are saying online— identifying whether the conversation around your brand is positive, neutral, or negative. This combination of direct and indirect feedback methods gives a more comprehensive view of how your brand is perceived, allowing you to pivot strategies when needed.

Tracking referral traffic and sales through discount codes or tracking links is another pivotal approach. Promotional codes add a layer of measurement to your campaigns by showing exactly how many conversions have resulted from influencer efforts. Each influencer can be provided with unique codes, granting you detailed insights into individual performance. Tracking links similarly allow you to monitor the flow of potential customers to your site, providing data on which influencers are driving visits and where these visitors land on your site. This quantifiable data is invaluable when determining the ROI of your partnerships and identifying which strategies are most effective at boosting sales.

Adjusting strategies based on performance data ensures your influencer marketing remains dynamic and aligned with your business goals. One practical method is A/B testing, which involves altering one element within two different advertisements to see which performs better. For example, you might test different call-to-action phrases or visuals to determine what resonates more with your audience. Through continuous testing and iteration, you can refine both content and choice of partners to ensure maximum effectiveness in reaching and converting your target audience.

Strategic adaptation requires flexibility, so don't shy away from making changes mid-campaign if current tactics aren't yielding desired results. It's vital to remain agile, exploring new approaches or even reconsidering partner selection based on ongoing insights. The ultimate goal isn't just to succeed in one campaign but to create a framework for future successes by understanding what works and why.

For small businesses with limited budgets, leveraging these strategies effectively can lead to substantial growth without breaking the bank. Whether you're aiming for increased brand awareness, higher sales, or both, consistently evaluating and refining your influencer marketing strategies will encourage better outcomes and make the most of your investment.

Bringing It All Together

As you wrap up this chapter, it's clear that tapping into the power of influencers can really amplify your business reach. By strategically identifying and collaborating with influencers who align with your brand values, you're positioning yourself to connect authentically with your target market. Remember, finding the right fit is crucial—think about what your brand embodies and look for influencers who naturally resonate with those traits. Whether you're promoting eco-friendly products or cutting-edge technology, aim for partnerships where the story feels genuine on both sides. But it doesn't stop at just finding the right influencer. Successful collaborations hinge on understanding their audience and how actively they engage with content. Demographics and engagement rates are key indicators of whether an influencer's followers will click with your offerings. And once you've established these connections, nurturing the relationships over time ensures lasting impact. Keep in mind that flexibility and continuous evaluation of your strategies based on real-world data will guide you toward effective and dynamic influencer marketing. This approach not only enhances immediate campaigns but also lays a solid foundation for future successes in the ever-evolving social media landscape.

Reference List

6 Email and Instagram DM Templates for Influencer Outreach. (n.d.). Brands.joinstatus.com. https://brands.joinstatus.com/influencer-outreach-templates

6 Helpful Tips for Influencer Relationship Management | GRIN. (2021, December 6). Grin.co. https://grin.co/blog/influencer-relationship-management/

Influencer Marketing Measurement: KPIs, Metrics, ROI. (2020, May 7). Meltwater. https://www.meltwater.com/en/blog/measuring-influencer-marketing

Influencer Marketing Focus Relationships. (n.d.). Business.com. https://www.business.com/articles/why-influencer-marketing-should-focus-on-relationships/

Sood, A. (2024, January 24). *10 metrics to track influencer marketing success in 2024*. Sprout Social. https://sproutsocial.com/insights/influencer-marketing-metrics/

Shopify. (2024, October 15). *How To Conduct Effective Influencer Outreach (2024) - Shopify*. Shopify. https://www.shopify.com/blog/influencer-outreach

Paid Advertising on Social Media

Paid Advertising on Social Media

Navigating the world of paid advertising on social media can seem like a daunting task, but it doesn't have to be. This chapter will guide you through the essentials of setting budget-friendly ad campaigns to enhance the visibility of your small business. Whether you're a small business owner, an entrepreneur, or a member of a marketing team, understanding how to make smart financial decisions for your advertising efforts is crucial. You'll discover that with some strategic planning, every dollar you invest can yield significant results, helping you reach and connect with more of the people who matter most to your business.

In the pages ahead, we'll delve into practical strategies for budgeting your ad spend wisely while exploring diverse ad formats tailored to different goals. You'll learn how to set effective cost-per-click (CPC) or cost-per-acquisition (CPA) targets, ensuring your campaigns remain viable and competitive. Additionally, we'll discuss maximizing impact with minimal spending by harnessing the power of retargeting ads and A/B testing. You'll also gain insights into keeping up with industry trends and using analytics tools to track performance. Through this chapter, you'll equip yourself with the knowledge needed to run successful ad campaigns that are both cost-effective and powerful in driving sales and engagement.

Setting Budget-Friendly Ad Campaigns

When you're diving into the world of paid advertising on social media, it can feel overwhelming. Don't worry; with a little planning and strategy, you can make every dollar count. One of the first steps is understanding your budget, which is crucial for small businesses looking to enhance visibility without breaking the bank.

Understanding Your Budget

First off, it's vital to get a clear picture of your current financial situation. Assess how much you can realistically allocate to ad spending. This involves reviewing your existing finances and setting a specific budget solely for advertisements. By doing this, you'll manage resources more effectively and avoid overspending. Remember, your goal is to balance between what you can afford now and how much return you expect from these efforts later.

Next, let's talk about choosing the right ad type. Social media offers a variety of ad formats—images, videos, carousels, and stories—that each come with their own costs and benefits. But how do you decide which one fits your goals and budget? It all starts with identifying what you want to achieve. If your aim is brand awareness, video ads might be your best bet due to their engaging nature. On the other hand, if driving traffic to a website is your target, carousels could work better as they showcase multiple products or services in a single swipe.

Here's a quick guideline: test different formats initially with a minimal budget. See which ones resonate most with your audience, then funnel more money into those. This method helps you learn where your investments yield the highest returns before committing large portions of your budget.

Setting Up Cost-Per-Result Goals

Another critical aspect is setting realistic CPC (Cost Per Click) or CPA (Cost Per Acquisition) targets. These metrics help you gauge whether your ads are performing well. Look at industry standards to understand average costs within your sector. This gives you a benchmark, ensuring your campaigns remain financially viable. To illustrate, suppose the average CPC in your industry is $1.50. Aim for a figure around this mark or lower to keep your campaigns competitive.

Review these targets regularly. Consider adjusting them based on the performance data you collect over time. Flexibility here is key. As your campaigns evolve, so too should your expectations and strategies, adjusting for any changes in market conditions or business objectives.

Maximizing Impact with Minimal Spend

A fantastic way to maximize your advertising impact without inflating costs is by leveraging retargeting strategies. Retargeting allows you to reconnect with users who have previously interacted with your brand but didn't convert. This tactic often leads to higher conversion rates because it targets people already familiar with and interested in your offerings. Best of all? Retargeting typically comes at no extra cost to your initial outreach efforts.

To implement effective retargeting, monitor audience insights closely. Platforms like Facebook and Instagram provide analytics tools that help you understand user behavior. Use these insights to refine your approach, honing in on segments that show higher engagement rates. For instance, if you notice a particular age group consistently interacts with your stories, consider creating more content tailored to their preferences.

Moreover, don't forget the power of A/B testing. Continually test variations of your ads—whether that's changing visuals, copy, or call-to-action prompts. Track which combinations deliver the best results and use that knowledge to optimize future campaigns.

Lastly, remember that learning never stops. Keep abreast of industry trends and updates on ad platforms. Regularly educate yourself on new features or algorithm changes that could impact your campaigns. Staying informed will help you adapt swiftly, maintaining efficiency and effectiveness in your advertising endeavors.

Target Audience Specification for Maximized ROI

Alright, so let's dive right in on how to identify and target the right audience for your social media ad campaigns. When you're a small business owner or entrepreneur just getting started with social media advertising, understanding who exactly your audience is can set the stage for successful campaigns.

First up, creating a detailed customer profile using demographic data is like setting up a blueprint for who you want to reach. Think of it as painting a picture of your ideal customer. Consider factors like age, gender, location, income level, and education. But don't stop there. Dive deeper by looking at interests, behaviors, and values. For instance, if you're selling eco-friendly products, you're probably targeting consumers who are environmentally conscious and value sustainability.

Developing these profiles isn't just about making guesses though. Use any existing customer data you have — maybe from past sales or website analytics. If you've got a brick-and-mortar store, think about who's walking through your doors most often. Gathering this data might seem tedious, but knowing your audience helps you craft messages that resonate and prompts actions like clicks and purchases.

Now, let's talk about utilizing platform tools, like the well-known Facebook Ads Manager, to achieve precise targeting. These tools have evolved to offer more than just basic demographic filters. You can now zero in based on user interests and online behavior, reaching people who are most likely interested in what you offer. Say you run a local cafe; with Ads Manager, you could target users who frequently check into cafes nearby, engage with food photography, or follow related pages.

It's essential to explore all features available. Facebook Ads Manager, for example, allows for incredibly detailed targeting options — from broad categories like lifestyle and entertainment to niche ones like specific hobbies and travel interests. The tool's strength lies in its capacity to combine different targeting layers, which means you're capable of creating a highly specific target audience. Remember, the beauty of digital ads is their flexibility, allowing you to refine and tweak your settings as you gather more insights.

Experimentation is key when it comes to targeting. This is where split testing, also known as A/B testing, comes into play. It involves running two or more versions of your ads simultaneously to see which performs better with your audience. Maybe you test variations in copy, imagery, or even audience segments. For instance, if you're unsure whether to focus on a younger vs. older demographic, split testing lets you trial both with a small budget, then scale up investment in the best-performing option. Over time, these tests guide optimizations leading to higher conversion rates.

Don't be afraid to try out different combinations either. Test different geographic areas, interests, and even purchase behaviors. Sometimes, the results can surprise you, revealing untapped market segments you hadn't initially considered. This method not only boosts your current campaign's effectiveness but also builds a repository of data for future strategies.

Once your campaign is live, regularly updating and refining your audience profiles is crucial. Let performance feedback and engagement metrics be your guide. Pay attention to which audiences are engaging the most and converting. Are certain age ranges consistently clicking through more? Maybe one interest group shows a much higher affinity for your product. Use this data to continually adjust your audience parameters for optimal results.

Metrics like click-through rates, engagement levels, and conversion statistics aren't just numbers; they tell a story about your audience's preferences and habits. Suppose an ad targeted at city-dwellers underperforms compared to one aimed at suburban residents, this insight should prompt a reassessment of your urban strategy.

Staying attuned to performance doesn't mean changing things daily, but having a schedule to review and adapt ensures you're not pouring your marketing dollars into ineffective strategies. Perhaps consider weekly or bi-weekly reviews depending on your ad spend and campaign duration. Each assessment offers a chance to refresh and refine, ensuring alignment with your evolving business objectives and market changes.

Analyzing Ad Performance

Engagement metrics are a treasure trove of insights that, if interpreted correctly, can revolutionize how you target your paid advertisements. These metrics—such as likes, comments, shares, clicks, and conversions—give small business owners a window into their audience's behavior and preferences. The key is to determine whether your ads are reaching the right people. For example, if an ad receives many clicks but few conversions, it may be reaching a broad audience rather than a targeted one. Conversely, high engagement rates indicate that the ad resonates well with its intended audience.

Understanding these patterns allows for strategic adjustments in both content and targeting efforts. It's vital to regularly monitor these analytics to refine your advertising strategies continuously. This isn't just about maximizing ad spend efficiency; it's about ensuring that every dollar spent contributes to meaningful engagement and, ultimately, sales.

Feedback from your audience is another invaluable resource when it comes to fine-tuning ad content. The digital landscape allows audiences to interact with brands in real-time, offering immediate feedback through comments, reactions, or messages. Being attentive to this feedback helps in assessing public perception and relevance. When an ad sparks conversations or receives repeated queries, it might be an opportunity to dive deeper into what aspects are resonating or missing the mark.

Let's say there's a recurring comment about clarity or product details being insufficient. This suggests an area for improvement in future campaigns. By adapting content based on this feedback, businesses not only maintain their relevance but also increase engagement levels by showing they listen to their audience. This adaptability fosters stronger connections with current and potential customers, enhancing brand loyalty over time.

Taking full advantage of analytics tools can propel a business's understanding of market trends and customer behaviors far beyond basic ad performance. Many social media platforms offer built-in analytics, but investing in specialized third-party tools can amplify insights. These tools aggregate data across various channels into comprehensive dashboards, revealing trends that inform future targeting strategies (West, 2021).

For instance, using advanced analytics like those provided by Sprout Social or Google Analytics, businesses can access deep insights into demographics, user interests, and geographic locations. These insights guide more precise ad targeting, enabling a sharper focus on segments likely to convert. Tools equipped with capabilities such as A/B testing within Facebook Ads Manager allow advertisers to easily experiment with different audience segments or ad formats, pinpointing what resonates best (Socinova, 2023).

Every campaign should be viewed as a learning experience. This mindset ensures continual improvement in advertising methods. After a campaign ends, it's important to conduct a thorough analysis of what worked and what didn't. Was the timing optimal? Did one ad perform significantly better than others? Answering these questions helps refine future campaigns.

Documenting successes and failures builds a repository of knowledge that informs decision-making and strategy formulation. Small businesses, often operating with tighter budgets, can particularly benefit from this iterative approach. With each campaign, new insights emerge, helping to sculpt more effective and efficient advertising strategies moving forward.

Incorporating these practices into your advertising strategy creates a cycle of constant evaluation and enhancement. By interpreting engagement metrics, responding to feedback, leveraging analytics tools, and learning from each campaign, small businesses can optimize their ad targeting effectiveness. This proactive approach ensures ongoing relevance in a competitive marketplace, driving increased visibility and sales.

Summary and Reflections

Effectively utilizing paid advertisements can be a game-changer for small businesses aiming to enhance visibility and drive sales. In this chapter, we've explored budget-friendly ad campaigns, emphasizing the importance of understanding your financial limits and selecting the right ad types tailored to your goals. By setting realistic cost-per-result targets and regularly reviewing them, you ensure that your campaigns remain competitive and financially viable. We've also highlighted maximizing impact with minimal spend through strategies like retargeting and A/B testing. These methods help in fine-tuning your ads for better engagement without overspending.
Targeting the right audience stands as another cornerstone for boosting your return on investment. Crafting detailed customer profiles and leveraging tools like Facebook Ads Manager allows you to precisely reach potential buyers who align with your product or service. Through experimentation and continual adjustments based on performance metrics, you gain valuable insights into what resonates with your audience. This ongoing process of learning and adapting ensures your advertising efforts are not just efficient but also effective in capturing the attention of those most likely to convert. Keep honing

your strategies, stay updated with market trends, and never stop tweaking your approach to maintain relevance and drive success in your marketing journey.

Reference List

Goeser, M. (2024, April 10). *Marketing Director's Guide to Maximizing Your Google Ads Budget*. Augurian. https://augurian.com/blog/google-ads-budget-allocation-guide/

Gillin, G. (2024, January 25). *Cost-Effective Strategies for Meta Ad Campaigns: Optimizing Your Advertising Budget - By Garrett Gillin - 215 Marketing*. 215 Marketing. https://215marketing.com/resources/cost-effective-strategies-for-meta-ad-campaigns-optimizing-your-advertising-budget-by-garrett-gillin/

How to Use Facebook Audience Insights for Better Targeting. (2018, March 16). Sprout Social. https://sproutsocial.com/insights/facebook-audience-insights/

SaveMyLeads. (2024, June 17). *How to Set Demographics in Facebook Ads | SaveMyLeads*. SaveMyLeads. https://savemyleads.com/blog/other/how-to-set-demographics-in-facebook-ads

Socinova. (2023, November 6). *5 Top Analytical Tools To Boost Ad Campaign Performance in 2024*. Socinova. https://socinova.com/analytical-tools-ad-campaigns/

West, C. (2021, March 26). *10 of the Best Social Media Analytics Tools for Brands*. Sprout Social. https://sproutsocial.com/insights/social-media-analytics-tools/

Case Studies in Success

Case Studies in Success

Success stories in social media marketing often serve as powerful guides for anyone looking to make a splash in the digital space. Learning from businesses that have already navigated these waters can provide both inspiration and practical insights. This chapter dives into an array of real-world examples where innovative use of social media led to remarkable business outcomes. Different industries have utilized various platforms uniquely, showcasing how creativity combined with strategic planning can drive significant sales growth and brand visibility. Whether you're a small business owner, an entrepreneur just starting out, or a marketing professional seeking fresh ideas, these case studies offer more than just theoretical knowledge; they present tested strategies that have proven effective in the challenging yet rewarding world of social media.

As we embark on this journey, be prepared to uncover the secrets behind successful campaigns across diverse sectors. From using Instagram to attract foot traffic to cafes and employing Facebook's tools to streamline fundraising efforts, you'll explore how each story holds valuable lessons for different business contexts. The chapter also highlights the critical role of understanding platform-specific trends and audience behaviors to harness the full potential of social media channels. With a focus on actionable takeaways, these case studies will equip you with the knowledge to adapt these approaches to your circumstances. So get ready to learn how these companies turned likes and shares into tangible success, and discover how you too can replicate these wins in your own ventures.

Breakdown of Successful Campaigns

As we delve into real-world examples of successful social media campaigns, the aim is to uncover what makes them tick and see how small businesses can replicate these strategies for their own growth. Let's start by examining a small online retail business that ran an exceptionally well-executed holiday campaign.
Operating on a tight budget, this business smartly harnessed the power of social media to engage their audience effectively during the bustling holiday season. They used targeted ads on platforms like Facebook and Instagram, carefully crafted with vibrant visuals and compelling offers tailored to appeal to their specific audience demographic. By scheduling posts and ads at peak times when their audience was most active, they

maximized engagement without overspending. A key takeaway here is the importance of understanding your audience's behavior patterns and using analytics to track which content formats and posting times yield the highest returns. For small businesses, it's crucial to allocate resources where they will have the most impact, ensuring every dollar spent contributes directly to visibility and sales growth.

Next, let's discuss how a local café successfully increased foot traffic through strategic use of Instagram. This café focused on building a robust brand presence by sharing high-quality images of their dishes, cozy ambience, and happy customers enjoying meals. They frequently posted about special promotions, such as limited-time discounts or seasonal menu items, which sparked curiosity and drew new patrons through their doors. The café also engaged actively with their community by responding promptly to comments and encouraging user-generated content. By inviting customers to share their own photos and experiences using branded hashtags, the café fostered a sense of community and loyalty, turning satisfied customers into ambassadors for their brand. To emulate this, businesses should focus on creating visually appealing content that resonates with their target market and encourages interaction, building genuine connections with their followers.

Another impactful strategy comes from a non-profit organization that leveraged Facebook to drive donations during a fundraising campaign. They crafted emotionally engaging stories that highlighted the direct impact of donations, using videos and written narratives that featured beneficiaries and the causes supported. By tapping into the emotional aspect of giving, they were able to communicate their mission clearly and motivate people to contribute. The organization also made good use of Facebook's fundraising tools to create a seamless donation process, allowing supporters to easily share the campaign within their networks. Engaging volunteers and advocates to share personal stories related to the cause further amplified their reach and authenticity. This approach underscores the value of storytelling in making campaigns relatable and inspiring action. Non-profits—and indeed any business—should consider how they can present their message in ways that are not only persuasive but also deeply personal.

For each of these case studies, a few guidelines emerge that can be adapted by businesses looking to develop effective social media strategies. First, it's essential to define clear objectives for your campaign; knowing what you want to achieve guides every decision and ensures consistency in messaging. Second, always tailor your content to suit the platform and audience. Each social media channel has its own unique culture and technical requirements—what works on Instagram may not work on LinkedIn or Twitter. Finally, measure and adapt. Use analytics to review your success metrics regularly, which allows you to refine your strategies and stay responsive to audience feedback.

Lessons Learned from Diverse Industries

In today's digital age, the ability of businesses to harness social media for sales and marketing is not just a trend—it's a necessity. Let's dive into some inspiring case studies from various industries that have masterfully adapted social media for their selling strategies. These examples will highlight universal principles that can benefit any business, regardless of its field.

First, let's look at the story of a tech startup that tapped into LinkedIn's vast potential to enhance their B2B sales. The company recognized that LinkedIn is more than just a platform for job seekers; it's a goldmine for professional networking. By strategically building and engaging with a network of relevant industry contacts, the startup was able to generate high-quality leads. But they didn't stop there. They bolstered their credibility by sharing thought leadership content, such as insightful articles and white papers, which positioned them as experts in their niche. This approach not only attracted new clients but also helped sustain long-term relationships by continuously adding value to their connections.

For small tech firms looking to replicate this success, it's essential to focus on cultivating genuine interactions rather than solely pushing sales messages. Businesses can start by optimizing their profiles with clear messaging and engaging content, then consistently share industry insights and updates that spark meaningful conversations. Engaging with your audience and providing educational content can help establish your brand as a trusted resource within the community, making it more likely for potential clients to consider your services when needed.

Switching gears to the fitness sector, we find brands thriving on Instagram and YouTube by fostering an environment of trust and education. A leading fitness brand effectively utilized these platforms to elevate their consumer engagement. On Instagram, the brand showcased product highlights visually, appealing directly to fitness enthusiasts who seek authentic reviews before purchasing equipment or apparel. Complementing this strategy, they partnered with fitness influencers who shared personal stories about using their products, offering a relatable perspective to followers. Meanwhile, on YouTube, the brand produced educational workout videos, ranging from beginner guides to advanced training sessions, which further cemented their authority in the fitness industry.

Fitness brands wanting to follow in these footsteps should prioritize creating informative and visually appealing content. Establish relationships with influencers whose values align with your brand, as their endorsements can significantly sway purchasing decisions. Additionally, consistent posting schedules and interactive campaigns, like Q&A sessions or live workouts, can foster a community feel, encouraging customer loyalty.

Moving into the fashion world, a sustainable clothing brand found its niche through Pinterest's unique visual focus. Understanding that Pinterest thrives on stunning imagery, the company curated boards catering to different style segments, such as eco-friendly formal wear or casual staples. They skillfully employed seasonal trends to keep their content fresh and relevant, ensuring ongoing engagement with their audience. This strategic use of Pinterest not only increased their brand visibility but also drove traffic to their website, where users could make purchases directly after viewing inspiration on their pinboards.

Fashion and lifestyle brands can leverage Pinterest by developing a nuanced understanding of their target market and using this knowledge to create compelling, themed collections. Staying current with emerging trends and being willing to adapt quickly can maximize engagement and turn casual browsers into committed buyers. Brands should focus on regularly updating their boards with high-quality images and branded visuals that resonate with their audience's interests and aesthetics.

Leveraging Platform-Specific Trends

As you dive into the world of social media marketing, it's fascinating to see how different brands have harnessed unique aspects of various platforms to elevate their visibility and engagement. One striking example is a subscription box service that saw its fortunes change overnight thanks to the viral potential of TikTok. This platform's emphasis on short-form content and trend-driven creativity played in favor of the brand when one of their videos went viral, catapulting their visibility and sales to new heights. What started as a simple showcase of their product quickly captured the imaginations of a vast audience, resulting in increased brand recognition and an uptick in subscriptions. TikTok's algorithm is adept at pushing engaging content to a broader audience, especially if it resonates with current trends or offers something fresh and entertaining. The key takeaway here for small business owners and entrepreneurs is the importance of tapping into the dynamic nature of TikTok by understanding its pulse—keeping content trendy, authentic, and visually appealing. It is not merely about creating videos but crafting stories that connect with the platform's predominantly young and vibrant audience. Integrating humor, authenticity, and creativity could significantly increase a brand's chances of going viral, providing a substantial return on investment in terms of exposure and customer reach.

Moving on to a different platform, Facebook provides another compelling case study with real estate agencies utilizing its versatile features. During the surge in demand for virtual interaction brought about by recent global events, a real estate agency adopted Facebook Live tours to offer virtual property showings. By doing so, they enabled prospective buyers to explore listings interactively from the comfort of their homes. These live tours were not mere walkthrough videos; they were enriched with real-time Q&A sessions, allowing potential buyers to ask questions and receive answers instantly. This interactive element not only enhanced viewer engagement but also fostered a sense of connection between the agent and the audience.

The agency's strategy capitalized on Facebook's extensive reach and real-time capabilities, creating a more accessible and engaging experience for homebuyers. For small businesses looking to implement similar strategies, leveraging Facebook Live could be a cost-effective way to conduct virtual events, product launches, or informational sessions. It's crucial to prepare thoroughly, ensuring your presentation is informative, engaging, and addresses common queries from your target audience. By transforming viewers into active participants, businesses can cultivate a community feeling and drive shareability of content, expanding their reach organically through viewer interactions.

Finally, influencer partnerships on TikTok illustrate another powerful approach to boosting brand awareness. A company collaborated with popular TikTok influencers to promote their products, taking advantage of the influencers' established followings and credibility with audiences. These influencers crafted engaging content around the brand's offerings, often incorporating them naturally into their usual style and themes, making the promotions feel authentic rather than forced. The impact was immediate and significant, driving rapid increases in brand awareness and consumer interest due to the influencers' strong connections with their followers.

For startups and entrepreneurs, this underscores the potential of partnering with influencers who align well with your brand's values and target demographic. Selecting the right influencers involves careful research into their audience demographics, engagement rates, and content style. Ideally, the collaboration should feel genuine and provide value to both the influencer's audience and the brand. Additionally, fostering long-term relationships with influencers can lead to sustained engagement and brand loyalty even beyond initial promotional activities.

Wrapping Up

This chapter has taken us on a journey through various social media success stories, showcasing how different businesses have creatively used these platforms to boost their visibility and sales. From small online retailers working with tight budgets to local cafés building community loyalty, each example highlights the power of understanding and engaging your audience. For small businesses and entrepreneurs, it's all about crafting the right content at the right time, whether that's using eye-catching visuals or tapping into emotional storytelling to drive engagement and results. We've also explored specific industries like tech startups and fitness brands, revealing how they leverage individual platforms such as LinkedIn, Instagram, and YouTube to connect with their audiences. These stories show that regardless of industry, focusing on authenticity, interaction, and strategic use of platform features can significantly benefit your brand. Whether you're inspired to host virtual tours on Facebook Live or jump into TikTok's trend wave, remember that staying flexible and audience-focused is key. As you step into your own social media endeavors, keep these insights in mind to craft strategies that resonate and succeed.

Reference List

Baker, M. (2023, August 3). *Viral Social Media Marketing Campaigns by Small Businesses*. ZD Blog. https://www.zilliondesigns.com/blog/viral-social-media-marketing-campaigns-by-small-businesses/

Moreno, L. (n.d.). *Top 10 Brands Killing It on Instagram - Social Media Strategies Summit Blog*. https://blog.socialmediastrategiessummit.com/top-10-brands-killing-it-on-instagram/

Siu, E. (2017). *11 Companies That Are Killing It with Their Digital Marketing Campaigns*. Convince and Convert: Social Media Consulting and Content Marketing Consulting. https://www.convinceandconvert.com/digital-marketing/killing-it-with-digital-marketing-campaigns/

Social Media Marketing Guide for Restaurants + Examples of Restaurant Social Media Marketing (2024). (2019, May 24). Toasttab.com. https://pos.toasttab.com/blog/on-the-line/examples-of-awesome-restaurant-social-media-marketing?srsltid=AfmBOoqIIoRUpNpmuMVI-MEjzx-phkn2iqrVjjeM1XRmqBIPGFmrEsUG

Sharma, A. (2024, May 2). *7 Social Media Strategy Examples and How to Implement Them*. Sprinklr.com; Sprinklr. https://www.sprinklr.com/blog/social-media-strategy-examples/

Top 5 Social Media Sites | Informatics Inc. (n.d.). All Things Internet | Informatics Inc. https://www.informaticsinc.com/blog/2013/5-popular-social-media-sites-and-companies-using-them

Future-Proofing Your Strategy

Future-Proofing Your Strategy

In a world where social media is constantly evolving, future-proofing your strategy is about embracing adaptability. The digital landscape changes at a breakneck pace, and staying ahead requires an open-minded attitude toward new tools and trends. Small business owners, entrepreneurs, and marketing professionals need to be ready for anything the future might throw their way. Whether it's integrating AI into customer interactions or exploring augmented reality experiences, flexibility is key. By remaining adaptable, businesses can navigate the complex terrain of social media marketing and ensure sustainable growth as technologies continue to advance.

This chapter delves into how small businesses can prepare for upcoming shifts in social media and marketing environments. You'll explore how AI-powered tools such as chatbots can enhance customer service and marketing efforts while offering round-the-clock support. Discover the benefits of predictive analytics, augmented reality, virtual reality, and how these technologies can transform customer experiences and optimize marketing strategies. Learn about the rise of social commerce integration, which allows seamless shopping directly through social media platforms. We'll discuss the transparency and security that blockchain brings to transactions and how it can boost consumer trust. Additionally, this chapter offers insights on assessing your business needs and resources when adopting these innovations, ensuring you choose the right technology to align with your goals. With practical advice tailored for small businesses and startups, you'll gain valuable knowledge to effectively use emerging social media technologies for maximum impact and brand success.

Emerging Technologies in Social Media

In today's rapidly changing digital world, small business owners must be aware of the latest innovations in social media technology to effectively integrate these advancements into their sales strategies. Among these innovations, AI-powered tools play a pivotal role by enhancing customer service and marketing efforts. Take chatbots, for example. These AI-driven assistants provide 24/7 support, ensuring that customers receive immediate assistance regardless of time zones or business hours. This continuous availability not only improves customer satisfaction but also boosts engagement levels.

Moreover, AI tools offer more than just customer interaction—they can optimize marketing strategies through predictive analytics. By analyzing customer data and predicting future behaviors, AI enables businesses to create personalized messaging tailored to individual preferences. Imagine being able to send a message to a customer about new products based on their previous purchases. This level of personalization increases the likelihood of conversion, making marketing campaigns more effective.

Moving beyond AI, Augmented Reality (AR) and Virtual Reality (VR) technologies are transforming how customers experience shopping. These tools add an immersive layer to online shopping by allowing users to visualize products in their real environment before purchasing. For instance, AR can enable a shopper to see how a piece of furniture might look in their living room, while VR can offer a full-fledged virtual store tour or product demonstration. Initiatives like virtual try-ons not only engage customers but also reduce return rates by helping them make informed decisions.

Such immersive experiences foster deeper connections between consumers and brands. Interactive AR campaigns can drive brand storytelling, while VR-driven experiences can showcase product highlights in innovative ways. Brands that embrace these technologies can capture the attention of tech-savvy audiences who value unique and engaging interactions over traditional static content.

Another emerging trend reshaping the landscape is social commerce integration. Social media platforms have evolved from being mere networking sites to comprehensive shopping destinations. By incorporating shopping features directly within these platforms, businesses can leverage the power of social commerce to facilitate impulse buying. Users browsing Instagram or Facebook can now purchase products without being redirected to external websites, creating a seamless transition from discovery to purchase.

This ease of access significantly enhances the consumer experience and boosts conversion rates. For small businesses with limited resources, social commerce provides a cost-effective alternative to traditional e-commerce setups, leveling the playing field in competitive markets. Entrepreneurs can harness these built-in shopping tools to reach wider audiences and maximize their reach without extensive investment in complex e-commerce infrastructures.

Blockchain technology further enriches the realm of innovation by introducing transparency and security in transactions. Particularly appealing to ethically-conscious consumers, blockchain ensures that all transactions are secure and transparent. Its decentralized nature prevents fraud, offering peace of mind to both buyers and sellers. Additionally, blockchain's traceability can be leveraged to authenticate products and certify their origins, resonating well with consumers interested in sustainable and ethical sourcing.

Beyond transactional benefits, blockchain holds potential for enhancing trust across ecosystems. Businesses adopting blockchain can effectively manage supply chains, ensuring that every step of the process is visible and verifiable. This transparency fosters stronger relationships with partners and stakeholders by instilling confidence in practices and processes.

For business owners looking to implement these innovations, it's vital to start by understanding their specific needs and resources. Evaluate which technologies align best with your goals. With AI, consider investing in chatbots or predictive analytics tools to enhance personalized customer experiences. If aiming for immersive experiences, assess your readiness to incorporate AR or VR into your marketing. Social commerce may require aligning your current social media strategy with platform-specific shopping features.

When considering blockchain, understand the compliance requirements and potential collaborative opportunities within your industry. Cooperation with other businesses using blockchain can establish robust ecosystems that benefit all participants.

Adapting to Changes in Consumer Behavior

In today's fast-paced digital world, staying in tune with the shifting preferences and behaviors of consumers is crucial for small business owners. The ability to pivot strategies quickly, improve customer satisfaction, and ultimately drive growth hinges on understanding and acting upon these evolving consumer dynamics. Whether it's through feedback mechanisms, embracing sustainability, or catering to personalization and instant gratification, businesses must adapt to the changing landscape to ensure their long-term success.

Seeking and incorporating customer feedback is a vital practice that enables businesses to stay agile and responsive. Feedback serves as a direct line of communication with your target audience, providing insights into what works and what doesn't. By actively engaging with customers through surveys, online reviews, or even direct conversations, businesses can gather valuable information that helps them refine their products or services. For instance, a cafe might introduce a new menu item based on frequent customer requests, demonstrating how listening to customer voices can lead to tangible improvements. Incorporating feedback allows businesses to identify trends early and adjust their offerings accordingly, ensuring they remain relevant and desirable.

However, with great data power comes great responsibility. Implementing robust data security measures is crucial to maintain consumer trust and protect sensitive information. As consumers become increasingly concerned about privacy, businesses must ensure their data protection policies are airtight. A breach of trust can have lasting repercussions on a brand's reputation. For startups and small businesses, investing in cybersecurity solutions, like encryption and access controls, safeguards customer data against unauthorized access and reinforces trust.

As technology advances, the landscape of consumer expectations and behavior evolves. Businesses need to be agile, utilizing data effectively to remain relevant. Predictive analytics helps foresee and capitalize on changes, while understanding consumer behavior ensures that businesses meet their audience's needs. Data visualization simplifies strategic planning, translating raw numbers into clear insights. Meanwhile, upholding strong data security indicates respect for customer privacy and supports long-term relationships.

Bringing It All Together

As we've explored throughout this chapter, understanding and adapting to the evolving social media and marketing landscapes is key for small business owners. With innovations like AI-powered tools, AR, VR, and blockchain technology, there's a wealth of opportunities to enhance customer engagement and streamline operations. The beauty of these technologies is their ability to offer personalized experiences and foster genuine connections with consumers. By integrating such innovations thoughtfully, small businesses can enhance their market presence without breaking the bank. The goal is not just keeping up but thriving in an ever-changing digital world.
Looking ahead, it's essential to stay flexible and open to change. The landscape will continue to evolve, bringing new trends and challenges. Small businesses that adapt quickly by leveraging data-driven insights and staying attuned to consumer behavior are better positioned for success. Whether it's embracing social commerce or ensuring robust data security, these strategies help build trust and loyalty among customers. Remember, every technological advancement offers an opportunity for growth and innovation, so don't shy away from exploring them in your journey towards achieving business goals.

Reference List

Asia, A. (2024, October). *Understanding Consumer Behaviour in the Digital Era*. Ada-Asia.com; ADA Asia. https://www.ada-asia.com/resources/insights/consumer-behaviour-in-digital-era

Andrei Kholkin. (2024, August 15). *Data Driven Insights: Unlocking Business Potential with Analytics*. Weberlo.com. https://www.weberlo.com/blog/data-driven-insights

Insights, S. (2022, July 4). *Top 9 Social Technology Trends & Innovations in 2022*. StartUs Insights. https://www.startus-insights.com/innovators-guide/social-technology-trends/

PWC. (2022). *The Essential Eight Technologies*. PwC. https://www.pwc.com/us/en/tech-effect/emerging-tech/essential-eight-technologies.html

Understanding Consumer Behavior in the Digital Age. (n.d.). William & Mary. https://online.mason.wm.edu/blog/understanding-consumer-behavior-in-the-digital-age

Why is Business Data Analytics and Why is it Important? (n.d.). Www.calmu.edu. https://www.calmu.edu/news/data-analytics-in-business